Learning to Get Along®

Join In and Play

Cheri J. Meiners, M.Ed.
Illustrated by Meredith Johnson

free spirit
PUBLISHING®

Text copyright © 2017, 2004 by Cheri J. Meiners, M.Ed.
Illustrations copyright © 2017, 2004 by Free Spirit Publishing Inc.

Library of Congress Cataloging-in-Publication Data
Meiners, Cheri J., 1957–
        Join in and play / Cheri J. Meiners ; illustrations by Meredith Johnson.
            p. cm. — (Learning to get along)
Summary: Simple text discusses how to develop the skills to make friends and play with others. Includes role-playing activities.
    ISBN 1-57542-152-6
    1. Play—Juvenile literature. 2. Social skills—Juvenile literature. 3. Friendship—Juvenile literature.
[1. Play. 2. Social skills. 3. Friendship.] I. Johnson, Meredith, ill. II. Title.
GV1203.M37 2004
790—dc22

                                                                        200301987

ISBN: 978-1-57542-152-0

Reading Level Grade 1; Interest Level Ages 4–8;
Fountas & Pinnell Guided Reading Level H

Cover and interior design by Marieka Heinlen
Edited by Marjorie Lisovskis

25 24 23 22 21 20 19
Printed in China
R18860119

Free Spirit Publishing Inc.
6325 Sandburg Road, Suite 100
Minneapolis, MN 55427-3674
(612) 338-2068
help4kids@freespirit.com
www.freespirit.com

Dedication

To the princess of charm,
who bubbles with laughter
and affection,
Andrea Rose

Acknowledgments

I wish to thank Meredith Johnson for her beautiful illustrations. I also thank Judy Galbraith and all those at Free Spirit who believed in this series. Special thanks go to Marieka Heinlen for the lovely design and to Margie Lisovskis who, as editor, has contributed her wonderful expertise and creativity. Finally, I am grateful to Mary Jane Weiss, Ph.D., whose insight, skill, and caring have done much to advance the field of teaching social skills.

I like to play.

I can do lots of things alone.

Sometimes, I'd rather play with a friend.

When I see someone I'd like to play with,
I can walk up and smile as I say hello.

The person might be looking for
a friend, too.

I can tell something about me or ask a question.

What are you drawing?

I can listen.

I can answer in a nice way.

Sometimes my friend invites me
to play along.

I can also ask to play.

I might think of a way to join in.

When I ask to join in,
people might say no.

I can ask again later.

Or I can look for a different friend to play with me.

If I need help joining in
I can ask a grown-up.

I can invite someone to play with me.

I can tell my ideas
and listen to other ideas, too.

When we share ideas, we are cooperating.

I can play with more than one friend.

My friends can, too.

I want everyone to get along.

Sometimes I lose a game,
or get picked last,
or don't get a turn.

I can still have fun.

And things might go better next time.

When things don't go well for someone else, I can say something kind.

A person may do something
that I don't think is fair.

I can say how I feel.

If I also listen to how the other person feels, we may solve our problem.

I can play fair and follow the rules.

I can listen and speak kindly.

I can share and wait my turn.

I can show respect.

When I join in and play,
I can make friends by being a good friend.

Ways to Reinforce the Ideas in *Join In and Play*

As you read each page spread, ask children:

- What's happening in this picture?

Here are additional questions you might discuss:

Page 1

- What are some things you like to play when you're by yourself?

Pages 2–11

- What are some things you like to do with a friend?

- When you want to join in and play with someone, what can you do? *(Discuss ideas like saying hello; watching for a while to show interest and to figure out a way to join in; asking a question or starting a conversation; asking to play; and suggesting a way to join in. For example, on page 11, the girl might offer to turn the rope so the boy could jump.)*

- If you are playing and see someone who might like to join you, what can you do? What can you say?

Pages 12–13

- Is it ever okay to say no when someone wants to play with you? When are some times people might say no? What are some nice ways to say no?

- If you ask to join in and someone says no, what can you do?

- Do you think these children could have found a way to say yes? What could they have done?

Pages 14–15

- When might you need help joining in?

- Who are some grown-ups who can help you?

Pages 16–21

- Have you ever invited someone to play? What did you say?

- Why is it fun to play games with other people?

- What does it mean to cooperate? How are these children cooperating?

- What are some ways you cooperate when you play?

Pages 22–23

- How does this boy feel? What do you think he will do?

- Have you ever been sad because someone wouldn't play with you? What did you do?

Pages 24–27

- What problem do these children have? How did the children solve their problem?

- What can you do when you feel someone isn't being fair to you?

Pages 28–29

- What are these children doing to get along?

- What is respect? How does taking turns (following rules, playing fair) show respect? *(You might explain respect by saying, "When you show respect to people, you show that you think they are important.")*

Pages 30–31

- How are these children being good friends?

- Think about children you play with. How do they show that they are good friends?

- What can you do to be a good friend?

Join In and Play teaches beginning skills children can use to join and welcome others in play. Playing cooperatively is a complex activity for young children, involving a mix of skills and understandings. Observation helps children be aware of other people's actions, feelings, and needs. Cooperation begins when children are able to both assert themselves appropriately and develop a welcoming attitude toward others. Being a good sport teaches others to reciprocate. Playing fair involves several skills: following game rules, taking turns, sharing, listening, expressing feelings, speaking with kindness, cooperating, compromising, and solving problems.

Here are three guidelines you can use to support children as they develop skills for playing with others:

1. Watch and listen.

2. Ask and invite.

3. Play fair.

"Joining In" Games

Read this book often with your child or group of children. Once children are familiar with the book, refer to it when teachable moments arise involving both positive behavior and problems related to playing together. In addition, use the following activities to reinforce children's understanding of how to join together and play (adapting them as needed for use with a single child).

"Play" Practice

Preparation: Collect some toys and games to be used as props. On index cards, write prompts similar to the following. Place the cards in a bag.

Sample Prompts:

- Ask, "May I play with you?"
- Ask, "What are you doing?"
- Ask, "Can I have a turn?"
- Say, "That looks like fun."
- Ask, "Can I use that when you're done?"

- Ask, "Do you want a turn?"
- Ask, "Would you like to play with this now?"
- Ask, "What do you want to play?"
- Say, "You can go first."
- Ask, "Do you want to play with me?"

After a child draws a card, read or have the child read it aloud. Invite the child to choose a toy, approach a nearby child, and say what is on the card. The two children can then briefly act out a scene of joining in to play. Encourage the exchanges and play to continue for a short time, prompting and assisting as needed. The child who was approached can then draw the next card and approach a different child. Continue play until each child has had a turn drawing a card.

What Would You Do?

Present a play-related problem situation to children and discuss possible solutions with the whole group. Then break children into small groups of two to four. Tell each group to decide on one way to help solve the problem. Monitor how the groups are doing and help guide their discussions as needed. Allow groups three or four minutes to talk about the problem. Then have the small groups take turns telling their ideas to the whole group. Use the following examples of problems that occur during play (or make up your own).

Examples: Someone called someone else a mean name, tried to be the boss of the game, pushed another person who was in line for the slide, took something someone else was using, wanted to follow different game rules, left in the middle of a game.

Possible Solutions: Let children know that there are several appropriate responses. Among other choices, these might include: telling the person how you feel, ignoring what someone did, talking to an adult, thinking of a way to be friendly next time you see the person, calmly reminding the person of the rule, and smiling. Remind children that it is always best to "treat others as you want to be treated," and not to respond unkindly in return.